Toys Dolls & Teddy Bears

TOYS, DOLLS & TEDDY BEARS

MARSHALL CAVENDISH

❶ Under £5	❻ £100 – £250
❷ £5 – £10	❼ £250 – £500
❸ £10 – £20	❽ £500 – £1000
❹ £20 – £50	❾ £1000 – £5000
❺ £50 – £100	❿ Over £5000

To help give you an idea of the value of a particular piece, each item is price-guided at the end of its caption. Look at the number in the circle at the end of the caption and check it against the price guide key on this page. This will show you the price range into which the pictured item falls.

Every care has been taken to ensure that the information given in this book is correct. However, the prices of antiques are subject to fluctuation. The publishers do not accept any liability for financial or other loss incurred through information contained in this book.

This edition published by Bookmart Ltd,
Desford Road, Enderby, Leicester LE9 5AD

Produced by Marshall Cavendish Books
(a division of Marshall Cavendish Partworks Ltd)
119 Wardour Street, London W1V 3TD

First printed in 1996
Copyright © Marshall Cavendish Limited 1996

ISBN 1 85435 868 5

Printed and bound in Singapore

ONTENTS

COLLECTING TOYS, DOLLS & TEDDY BEARS

*MAGIC AND NOSTALGIA SURROUND CHILDHOOD
THINGS FROM ALL PERIODS OF HISTORY,
MAKING THEM A PERENNIAL FAVOURITE
AMONG COLLECTORS*

During the Victorian and Edwardian eras the growing realization that children were young people with individual needs and interests of their own served to inspire the creation of some of the most innovative toys and games that have ever been made – many of which have survived until today. Since that time, the mass production of toys has meant that the collector is faced with a constantly expanding choice of potential treasures.

As with other antique-collecting enthusiasts, collectors of childhood memorabilia tend to specialize in certain areas, favouring such items as teddy bears, bisque dolls, tin-plate toys, train sets or toy cars.

The *Antiques Pocket Guide* to *Toys, Dolls & Teddy Bears* will help you to establish the basic know-how needed to recognise period style and to understand some of the pitfalls involved in collecting. You are told exactly what to look for, how to avoid fakes and reproductions, and how to check for damage and repairs. The price guides give an idea of the current market value of these collectables. It is however as well to remember that their value can vary enormously from one area to another, depending on such factors as the condition and availability of an item, as well as the current fashion.

At the end of the day, however, the best advice is simply to buy what you like.

Happy Hunting!

BABIES' RATTLES

*IN GEORGIAN TIMES, THE RATTLE, ONE OF THE FIRST AND MOST
BASIC TOYS ANY CHILD EVER HAS, BECAME AN OBJECT OF
GREAT CRAFTMANSHIP AND VALUE*

I t seems that parents have always
known that being a tiny, helpless baby
can be a pretty boring affair. Ancient
Greeks and Romans realized that lying
around for hours on end, feeling their teeth
grow, made infants irritable. They attempt-
ed to beguile them with the simplest toy of
all, the rattle, which may date from even earlier times. Primitive rattles were made from
gourds or clay pots containing a stone or dried
pea. These poor efforts were discarded once
they outlived their usefulness.

Mediterranean peoples had long believed
that coral had magical properties and could
ward off evil spirits. New-born babies'
cradles were festooned with protective coral
beads. Soon, coral was being
used to make gum or
teething sticks to soothe
swollen gums and ward off evil

▼ *An elaborate
Regency rattle with
coral teething stick lies
alongside a bell marked
'baby', which is attached
to a length of ribbon.
The price guides read
from left to right.* **8** **5**

at the same time. Its hard, clean and cool surface was ideal for babies to gnaw on. It soon became common practice to present new-born babies with combination rattles and gum or teething sticks.

These christening presents became status symbols among the wealthier classes in Georgian times, and were made of gold or silver. Like other Georgian silver pieces, they were simply designed, with restrained decoration. They were valuable enough to be passed down as heirlooms. Georgian or Regency examples, complete with bells, a whistle and a coral or ivory teething stick, can be very expensive indeed.

Early Victorian rattles were more elaborate, and still incorporated bells, a whistle and a teething stick or ring. The Victorians, less impressed with the magical properties of coral, used mother-of-pearl, bone and ivory as alternative materials. Good examples will also be very expensive.

Later Victorian and early 20th century pieces are much more affordable. Silver and wood or tin rattles were being mass-produced, while synthetic materials, such as ivorine and celluloid, began to be used for handles and teething rings. Bells were now being replaced by moulded characters from childrens' books or animal shapes such as bears and rabbits.

Very early silver and gold rattles may not have a hallmark, but later examples will. Look for them on the mounts that hold the teething stick as this is the most likely spot to find them, though the makers' mark may be on the whistle. Clear, crisp hallmarks are best. Unmarked pieces are less desirable than marked ones.

▲ *A teething ring and a teething stick, both made of ivory, are found at either end of this handsome Victorian silver rattle.* ❼

◀ *The teething ring is ivory, attached to a silver rattle, while the late Regency rattle and whistle, with missing bells, has a mother-of-pearl handle.* ❺ ❻

DOLLS' HOUSES

DOLLS' HOUSES MAY BE THOUGHT OF AS MERE CHILDREN'S TOYS, BUT EARLY ONES ATTRACT THE ATTENTION OF ADULT COLLECTORS

Dolls' houses have fascinated children and adults alike for several centuries. Records of German dolls' houses go back as far as the 16th century. However, the earliest to survive the rigours of time is dated 1611. The fame of the German craftsmen soon spread all over Europe, and the English, French and Dutch soon began to make their own miniature houses and contents. Naturally, craftsmen modelled their work to reflect the fashions and tastes of their own particular time and place.

The best examples of really early dolls' houses often had decorations and furniture of such exquisite quality that it's obvious they were never meant for children to play with; they were intended for the delight of grown-ups. If eager little ones were ever allowed anywhere near them, it must have been under the closest supervision. Some houses were raised up on specially-made stands, well out of the reach of grubby little hands.

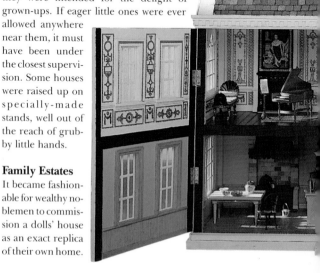

Family Estates

It became fashionable for wealthy noblemen to commission a dolls' house as an exact replica of their own home.

Some of these have survived, in their original condition, as family heirlooms which tell us a lot about the day-to-day lives of our ancestors. Their tastes and occupations and the organization of their homes are reflected in the details. Wallpaper, carpets, curtains, furniture and bric-a-brac all tell something about the people who made them and the person or persons who assembled the collection under one roof.

Very early dolls' houses – those made before about 1850 – tend to be one-off pieces and are priced accordingly. They usually end up in museums rather than private collections. However, succeeding generations of craftsmen have produced fine houses and furniture, and these are well worth looking into. Houses produced in the 1920s or 1930s are already taking on an 'antique' value. Twentieth-century dolls' houses are often made in the style

▼ This dolls' house is a beautiful Georgian reproduction. Genuine dolls' houses from that period are rare and prohibitively expensive.

*T*HE LONG HOUSE

'The Long House' was made around 1870, and is based on a traditional late Victorian suburban home. The standard of workmanship is very high, and although most of the rooms have been re-papered and re-carpeted the period feel is undisturbed. The house belongs to the National Trust.

of earlier houses, particularly Georgian ones. Among the more modern makers worth looking out for are Lines Brothers, who also traded as Triang, R. Bliss, Christian Hacker and the McLoughlin Brothers. The American manufacturer, Bliss, and the British one, Raphael Tuck, also made a fine selection of miniature shops, all fully stocked.

Small Worlds

Unfurnished houses tend to be cheaper than fully furnished ones. There is also a lot of fun to be had searching out suitable period furniture and other accessories, which should all be to scale. They are made in an enormous variety of materials. Look out for tin-plate pieces made by the German firm, Rock & Graner, Anglo-Indian pieces in carved bone, and, as a special indulgence, real silver miniatures. A. C. Lowe only stopped making furniture in 1985, but their fine craftsmanship

makes even relatively recent examples very collectable. Lines Brothers made dolls' houses and furniture up until the 1950s; later examples are often just as good, and no less sought after, as ones made by them in the 19th century.

Original Features

A house with all its original features intact is worth much more than one that has been 'improved'. This applies to a 1950s house just as much as to a classic of the 18th century. Scruffy but original wallpapers, curtains and fittings are more desirable than a refurbished interior, and the same applies to the outside.

Auctions are the best place to find desirable real estate, while specialist shops sell furniture and chattels. The size of most dolls' houses means that few people will have room for more than two or three, so choose carefully. Buying a dolls' house is like buying a real one; what really matters is that it appeals to you.

BISQUE DOLLS

DOLLS ARE POPULAR WITH LITTLE GIRLS OF ALL AGES AND THE CHILDHOOD COMPANIONS OF PREVIOUS GENERATIONS ARE MUCH SOUGHT AFTER BY COLLECTORS

The dolls of antiquity were simple wooden or pottery figures, but over the centuries different materials were used to produce ever more realistic dolls. In the 18th century, dolls' heads were made of wood, sometimes coated with gesso – a type of plaster of Paris – with the faces painted with the heavily rouged cheeks and beauty spots fashionable at the time. At the same time, moulded papier-mâché dolls were popular

▲ *These bisque-headed dolls are among the most beautiful playthings ever created. Their costumes imitate the layers of skirts, lace, bonnets and hats worn by their fashionable owners.*

𝒟EALERS' TIPS

- **Bisque heads are easy to damage and even the finest crack can drastically reduce a doll's value.**
- **Restoration can often be detected by feeling for a smoother area of bisque on the surface of a doll's body.**
- **Many reproductions are made from original moulds, and are of excellent quality, though the bisque is usually smoother in texture than earlier versions.**

because their features could be modelled more realistically. By the late 19th century, wax was also being used, though many a child lost her dolly by leaving it too close to the fireplace! By the 1860s and 70s, French manufacturers were making dolls with heads of bisque – an unglazed ceramic with a matt surface – and German doll makers were soon copying their designs.

The heyday of bisque dolls was from the mid-19th century to about 1930 and the manufacturers of Germany and France led the world in producing them. Germany was the most prolific producer and the Thuringia region of the former East Germany supported nearly 100 manufacturers at the industry's peak around the turn of the century. Many bisque heads from Germany were used by French makers, though the heads produced by the French themselves are often credited with being the most exquisite of all.

Few collectors' dolls are so keenly sought after as bisque-headed examples. But bisque is very fragile and heads often become casualties of accidents or rough use. If you want

▲ *The doll* (top) *with typically Edwardian clothes was made by Simon & Halbig, the other by Kestner.* ❼ ❻

▲ *Eyes that close when the doll is laid down work by a counterweight mechanism.*

▲ *The country of origin and the mould number are usually found on the back of the head.*

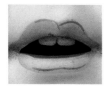

▲ *Most Edwardian dolls were made with open mouths that showed the teeth.*

to collect bisque dolls, therefore, it is vital to determine that the head is genuinely original, and this can be more easily established if you know something of the manufacturers and the marks they used. Most bisque dolls have information stamped on the back of the heads, usually under the wig.

German Dolls

Kestner & Co., established in 1805, is considered to be the founder of the doll industry in the Thuringia region. By 1823 it was producing dolls made of wax and papier mâché, and by 1888 ball-jointed bodies of cloth or leather were capped with high-quality bisque heads. In 1912 the highly successful all-bisque 'Kewpie' dolls appeared (the name is sometimes said to be a corruption of 'Cupid').

This doll was made in a variety of sizes but the larger ones, up to 43cm/17in, were fragile and are now very rare. After 1921, the company also made character dolls – these had heads which were not simply prettily stylized but were instead based on real-life faces.

Early Kestner heads were not marked, but dolls bearing the cipher X or XI are generally credited to the firm. In 1892 dolls were marked with 'Made in Germany' and had a mould number. In 1897 the Kestner alphabet marks were registered; these were on the head and read, for example, B/6, C/7, D/8 and so on. Sometimes, the initials of the founder J. D. Kestner were added to the other marks.

The firm of Gebrüder Heubach (Heubach Brothers) bought a porcelain factory in Thuringia in 1840. At first they made figurines and dolls' heads but by 1905 the company was producing complete dolls. Heubach heads were highly regarded and were often used by other doll manufacturers.

Armand Marseille was the most prolific of all German doll makers. After small beginnings, he too bought a porcelain factory in Thuringia and began to make bisque dolls' heads in 1890. The first heads made were mould number 390 and these are the most commonly found today. In 1901 'Floradora' dolls were made for George Borgfeldt in the USA. In 1919 the company amalgamated with Ernst Heubach and was known as the United Porcelain Factory of Koppelsdorf. The 'A M Dream Baby' appeared in 1924 and 'Baby Phyllis' doll in 1926.

Simon & Halbig were second only to Marseille as producers of dolls' heads in Germany. In the mid-1880s they issued heads with open mouths and moulded teeth. In 1893 the company began making oriental heads with real hair and were the most prolific producers of ethnic dolls in shades of yellow-gold to deep chocolate bisque. In 1920 the company was taken over by Kammer & Reinhardt.

Kammer & Reinhardt started business in 1886 and by 1890 were producing jointed dolls with bisque heads. The company became famous for its character 'baby' dolls and the first example was thought to be modelled on Kaiser Wilhelm's son. In 1902 the company began to use heads made by

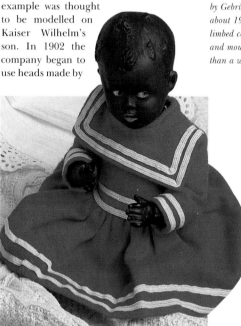

◀ *This baby doll, made by Gebrüder Heubach in about 1910, has a bent-limbed composition body and moulded hair rather than a wig.* ❾

▶ *This Kammer and Reinhardt toddler dates from c.1912 and bears mould number 122; it has a composition body and sleeping eyes.*

Simon & Halbig. In 1916, Kammer & Reinhardt merged with Bing of Nuremberg and in 1920 the firm took over Simon & Halbig.

French Dolls

Bru Jeune & Company was founded in Paris in 1866 and made fashion dolls in a variety of materials with bisque heads and shoulder plates. In 1867 a patented 'crying' doll and a 'laughing/crying' doll were issued. Later, in 1873, Bru made a doll with a swivelling

---

*M*ARKS

These marks are all from the top makers, including Kammer & Reinhardt, which used the mark (*above*) after the firm took over Simon & Halbig in 1920. 'S.F.B.J.' (*right*) stands for Société Française de Fabrication de Bébés et Jouets, founded by French makers in 1899 to combat German competition.

Armand Marseille
Germany
390
A 12 M

S. F. B. J.
60
PARIS

◀ *This delightful bent-limbed baby doll has a blonde wig. She is dressed in a traditional christening robe and lacy bonnet.* ❼

▼ *J.D. Kestner manufactured this character doll which bears mould number 260. The bisque head is made with sleeping eyes and an open mouth.* ❼

bisque head and bisque hands. Bébé Teteur, a doll that could suck liquids, was patented in 1879.

Pierre Jumeau of Paris first made fashion dolls noted for their elegant clothes. Portrait dolls, based on real children, appeared around 1870, and in about 1875, 'bébé' dolls appeared. These did not necessarily represent tiny babies but children from infancy to seven or eight years old.

Foreign Competition

By 1885 all Jumeau dolls carried the firm's trademarked name. Despite winning many gold medals for their fine dolls, Jumeau, like Bru, faced stiff competition from Germany and in 1899 both companies, along with other French manufacturers, amalgamated to form the S.F.B.J. – Société Française de Fabrication de Bébés et Jouets – to combat the threat. Demand for the society's products was high, but manufacturers still had to import some bisque heads from their German rivals. In 1957 the Society finally collapsed in the face of foreign competition.

EARLY CHESS PIECES

*POPULAR ALL AROUND THE WORLD, THE GAME OF
CHESS HAS INSPIRED CRAFTSMEN TO WHITTLE,
CARVE OR TURN A VARIETY OF ELEGANT FIGURES*

The game of chess is thought to have been invented in India in around the 6th century AD, though some believe it originated in China. The game passed from India to Persia, through the Islamic world, and from there into medieval Europe.

Originally the pieces were representational, usually based on animals. Later, the Moslems crafted their chess pieces in abstract shapes because it was forbidden for them to make images of men or animals. Due to a kind of Chinese whispers effect in translating names, the ones the Europeans gave the pieces were mostly quite different from the Persian and Indian originals; the Persian elephant, for example, became the *fou* (fool) in France and the bishop in England. Some terms are more directly related to their earlier languages; the ultimate object of the game, checkmate, is derived from the Persian words *shah*, meaning king, and *mat*, meaning dead.

▲ *This elegant king in
red-stained ivory was
shaped on a spinning
lathe. The cross at the
top and some decoration
in the middle were
carved by hand at a
later stage. The price is
for the set.* **8**

Chequered Board

Boards were originally uncoloured, but the familiar check pattern was in use by the 13th century. In the late 15th century European players altered the moves of the queen and the bishop to speed up the game, giving us, more or less, the game we know today.

Some chess sets were designed more as commemorative souvenirs than for actual use. The Napoleonic wars, for example, inspired a spate of sets in which the white and red (at this time more common than black) kings were busts or statuettes of the Duke of Wellington and

Napoleon. Every European country developed its own traditional designs, using different combinations of columns, balusters, discs, reels and finials.

▲ *This horn chess set was carved in the early 19th century in France.* ❼

Standard Designs

A lot of the Austrian and German sets from the 17th to the 19th centuries had characteristic tiers of pierced, spiky crowns (or 'crow's nests'), and double-headed knights. In England, sets were mostly either sturdy pieces on firm,

𝒟EALERS' TIPS

- Dating chess pieces over the last two centuries can be hard.
- With good quality ivory sets from the 19th century, the maker's name is very useful. It appears on the base of the white king (occasionally the red king as well).
- Names to look out for include **William Lund**, **Toy Brothers**, **G. Merryfield** and **John Jaques**.

*C*ANTONESE CHESS SETS

To cater for Georgian and Regency tastes for the exotic, the East India Company imported chess sets made in Canton. The sets that were produced for the West often portrayed European rulers on the white side. They were shown opposing Chinese and Manchu emperors. In this set, the white king represents George III while the queen is his wife, Queen Charlotte.

roughly hemispherical bases, or the more decorative 'barleycorn' pieces, balanced on a slender baluster rising from a flat disc.

Fed up with hearing the old 'I thought it was a bishop' excuse, 19th-century players decided to standardize the chess set, at least for serious tournament play. The elegant, well balanced pieces which eventually won this honour were designed by Nathaniel Cooke and manufactured by John Jaques of London. In 1849, they were given the blessing of the most important figure in the world of English chess, Howard Staunton. They have been known as 'Staunton' sets ever since.

Ivory Pieces

Ivory has traditionally been a favourite sub-
stance for making small sculptured objects that
have to be handled to be fully appreciated.
The finest ivory for chess pieces came from
the African elephant. Initially cream-coloured,
it turns yellow with age and is very smooth to
the touch. The best carving, though, was done
in the East, where the whiter ivory of the
Indian elephant was used. The white pieces
were usually left plain and the 'black' pieces
were stained red or green. Green is common
in Indian sets with lavishly decorated versions
of conventional pieces. Many magnificent or-
namental sets with the figures mounted on
elephants or riding in chariots were made in
India and China.

European carving was generally not as good
as Far Eastern workmanship, although sets
made in Dieppe (the centre of the French ivory
trade) can be outstanding.

Bone and Wood Sets

Bone was often used as a cheap alternative to
ivory. Many chess sets were turned and carved
in sheep's bone in the late 18th and early 19th
centuries. The best of these can now be as
valuable as similar ivory sets, notably those
carved by French prisoners of war in Napoleonic
times. However, by far the most common material was wood. The
best wooden sets used
boxwood for white pieces
and ebony for the black.
Top quality Staunton sets
have been made in weight-
ed boxwood and ebony
ever since John Jaques started producing them.

At the upper end of the
market, every conceiv-
able material has been
used for unusual or
luxury sets, including
bronze and silver.

▼▲ *These tall wooden
chess pieces belong to a
set made in Ireland for
the English nobility
around 1800. The price
is for the set.* ❿

PLAYING CARDS

CARDS OF ALL KINDS – ROUND OR RECTANGULAR, DECORATED WITH KINGS AND QUEENS OR WITH ACORNS AND BELLS – HAVE BEEN IN USE FOR HUNDREDS OF YEARS

▲ *The maker of this Edwardian pack of cards is identified on the ace of spades, as required since the 17th century.* ❷

N o one is absolutely sure where or when playing cards were invented, though it is thought they originated in China or India. They made their first appearance in Europe in the Middle Ages. However, cards were hand-painted and therefore only for the rich until the 15th century, when woodcut printing techniques made them accessible to people of all classes.

▼ *These gaming chips are made of mother-of-pearl.* ❹

A Popular Pastime

By the 17th century the playing of card games was well established in England. The Worshipful Company of Makers of Playing Cards was granted a royal charter

in 1628. From that time on, all card makers were required to identify themselves on the ace of spades and to register their identifying marks with the company.

During the middle of the 17th century thousands of packs were destroyed by the Puritans, who disapproved of gambling. With the restoration of Charles II in 1660, card playing flourished again.

In 1832 Thomas De La Rue patented a method for colour printing which meant that playing cards could be mass-produced, and all sorts of new games were developed, many of which – such as whist, bridge and patience – are still played today.

During the Victorian era, games for children flourished, and card games were no exception. Designs were created that were often educational in intent, and featured such subjects as astronomy, geography and Roman emperors.

Pack of cards

Most playing cards are made of pasteboard, though after 1934 some were printed on plastic. Early European cards were larger – and often thicker – than modern ones, and usually square or oblong, though sometimes they were round or oval.

European packs of cards always have four different suits of 13 cards each. The suits used today in Britain and France – as well as

▲ *These unusual cards are from America and date from around 1875. Their shape made them difficult to use and therefore unpopular.* ❻

▼ *This German pack of cards shows the suits used in that country. They were made by Piatnik in the 1930s.* ❸

► *Although this set dates from the 1980s, the design – called Baroque and made by Piatnik – has been popular for years.* ❷

in the United States and Australia – probably originated in the 15th century in the French town of Rouen, where there was a thriving card industry. Instead of spades, diamonds, clubs and hearts, German cards show leaves, bells, acorns and hearts, and the Italians play with cards featuring swords, coins, batons and cups.

Cards from oriental countries are quite different. Indian cards are round, with eight or ten suits, while Chinese cards are narrow and rectangular. Early Persian cards were small rectangles, sometimes made of ivory, decorated with wild animals and dancing girls.

From early in the 19th century until about 1880, transformation cards were popular in Britain. In these, the number of hearts, clubs, spades and diamonds was incorporated into a specific design. Each card in the pack illustrated something different.

Cards were often used in gambling games. Counters and chips were common substitutes for money and

▼ *These cards come from the popular Victorian game, Questions and Answers.* ❹

*D*EALERS' TIPS

There were many changes in the design of British cards during the 19th century, and these can be useful for dating.
• **During the reign of George IV (1820-30), the baton of the Jack of Hearts was replaced by a feather.**
• **The backs of cards were plain white until about 1850.**
• **Court cards always showed a single standing figure until about 1850, when firms first printed double-headed packs.**
• **Machine cutting replaced hand cutting in 1870, and corners became rounded.**
• **From around 1880 the value of the card was printed in both top left and bottom right corners.**

were made in various materials, including mother-of-pearl, bone and ivory.

Collectable Cards

Cards wear out quickly and are discarded, so hardly any survive from before 1600 and packs from the 17th and 18th centuries can be quite valuable. But older cards are not necessarily dearer than more recent ones, and cards and accessories from the 19th and early 20th centuries are now highly collectable.

When buying cards, check that you have a complete set, not one made up of odd cards with identical designs but different dates. Check the details of the printer's imprint and the quality of the printing. The box – if there is one – should be in good condition.

Early De La Rue packs are highly collectable, as are early 19th-century packs by Grimaud of Paris and Piatnik of Vienna. Also look out for cards made by the British firms of Goodall & Son; Count & Sons; and Maclure, Macdonald and McGregor.

Complete packs of children's card games from the 19th and early 20th centuries in good condition are fairly rare and can make an excellent subject for a collection.

▼ *The shaker of this Edwardian cup and dice is made of cardboard and tin; the dice are made of imitation ivory.* ❷❷

MONEY BOXES

*DESIGNED TO ENCOURAGE CHILDREN TO SAVE THEIR PENNIES,
MONEY BOXES ARE AS ENCHANTING TO ADULT COLLECTORS TODAY
AS THEY WERE TO THE YOUNG VICTORIANS AND EDWARDIANS*

T hrift was a much-praised virtue during the 19th century and the business of saving was made especially attractive for children. American youngsters were encouraged by ingenious mechanical 'money-banks' designed to provide amusement in return for sacrifice. One such device involved placing a dime in George Washington's hand, pulling a lever and seeing him fling it into a tree. You could then retrieve it by opening the bottom of the tree-trunk. British children got less exciting models; their banks tended to be cheap pottery pigs or tin-plate pillar boxes.

Symbolism played an important part in money-box design. The pig, which was fattened up for Christmas and other festivals, hinted clearly at investment towards future prosperity. Meanwhile, castles and buildings painted to resemble banks lent an air of solidity and security to a child's savings.

Houses, animals, eggs, barrels, post-boxes – whatever the image, it could be fashioned into a money box. Attractive early Victorian examples were made of wood, but the strongest and most expensive were those made of cast iron. In between were Staffordshire china cottages, typically featuring a traditional country cottage flanked on either side by a man and a woman in rural dress. Later on, tin-plate came

▼*This cast iron mechanical bank of Uncle Sam is highly collectable.* **9**

into use. Even though they were woefully flimsy, they were so cheap to buy that they could easily be replaced.

Tin-plate banks come in an infinite variety of designs from simple containers costing a few pounds to mechanical banks selling for hundreds. As a general guideline, European and American models are more desirable than British ones. Germany produced amusing mechanical banks, sometimes incorporating a clockwork mechanism or a musical box, while France turned out miniature vending machines that repaid investors with a chocolate. One exception to this rule was the British firm of John Harper & Co., whose attractive mechanical banks are a collector's dream.

The highest prices are paid for American mechanical banks. Manufactured in cast iron from about 1870 to the early 1900s, they featured subjects such as acrobats, bucking horses, or a monkey on a barrel organ. Some were operated simply by the weight of a coin, while others required the pulling of a lever. Names to look out for include Shepherd Hardware Co. and J. & E. Stevens Co. of Cromwell, Connecticut, two American firms which had the highest output.

▲ *This tin-plate money box is disguised as a real book. There is a slot in the top for posting pennies and the hinged cover opens to get the money out.* ❹

ⅅEALERS' TIPS

• **Always be wary of too much dirt: many fake boxes of the bronze or brass type have been buried in the garden by unscrupulous dealers to make them look older.**
• **Never buy a money box that has been re-painted. Since originals fade with age, be wary of brightly coloured ones.**
• **Make sure you are not buying a biscuit tin with a slot cut into it – many biscuit and sweet manufacturers sold their products in tins which could then be used as money boxes: these are worth much less than the real thing.**

SCRAPBOOKS & CUT-OUTS

FILLING AN ALBUM WITH CUT-OUT PICTURES WAS A FAVOURITE OCCUPATION FOR CHILDREN AT THE END OF THE 19TH CENTURY

S crapbooks were first kept by ladies of leisure in the late 18th century. By the middle of the next century this genteel hobby had expanded to create a thriving market for specially produced printed scraps, which were pasted into handsomely bound books made for the purpose.

Many books alternated blank pages with printed or embossed ones. The pages were interleaved with tissue paper to protect the scraps and there was often a coloured title page with space for someone to write a dedication; filled scrapbooks were a popular gift. Albums were imported from Germany or made in Britain; the printer's name is usually to be found on the title page.

Sheets of ready-made scraps were sold. At first, they were cut out and coloured by hand, but ready-coloured scraps were produced as printing techniques developed through the 19th century. With the invention of steel plates, very rich colour work could be done quickly

▲ *Postcards and advertising material are put together in this interesting Victorian scrapbook. The embossed postcards would have been used in scrapbooks.* ❺ ❷

and cheaply. The sheets were embossed to give a three-dimensional effect, and treated to give them a glossy sheen.

By the turn of the century, making scrapbooks was a popular hobby, though by then largely confined to children. Not only readymade scraps found their way into the albums. Pasted alongside them were Christmas, Valentine and birthday cards, picture postcards, photographs, theatre programmes and advertising material.

Scrapbooks have a great deal of appeal for the collector. Well-made examples, perhaps with the odd water-colour painting alongside the cut-outs, are attractive objects in their own right, while more random collections of cards, tickets and pictures cut from magazines can provide a fascinating record of their period. Most of the scrapbooks you will find today date from 1870 to 1910. This was the heyday for scraps, when vast quantities were printed. At this time, most scrap was designed for young tastes: soldiers, ships and policemen for boys; flowers, fruits and cats for girls.

Coloured postcards became popular sources of scrapbook material around the turn of the century, and Edwardian albums feature motor cars and aeroplanes as they became commonplace objects.

▲ *This modern album has been used to display old scraps.* **5**

▲ *Bookmarks, often used in bibles, were also made from scrap.* **2**

ROCKING HORSES

ROCKING HORSES, WHICH ONCE GRACED THE NURSERIES
OF WELL-TO-DO VICTORIAN AND EDWARDIAN HOUSEHOLDS,
ARE EAGERLY SOUGHT BY TODAY'S COLLECTORS

The first rocking horses for children were probably made in the 17th century and were of a somewhat crude design, with a head and tail attached to solid semi-circular wooden rockers. The classic form of the rocking horse – a galloping steed on a pair of bow-shaped rockers – was devised in the late 18th century and remained the standard type right through to the 1880s. It is still the type most beloved of collectors.

These rocking horses were realistically carved and generally had pricked ears, an open mouth and flared nostrils. Some were painted, frequently as dappled greys, with black patches on the legs and black hooves. The nostrils, eyes, mouth and ears were picked out in colour, and some even had glass eyes. The most prized horses sported manes and tails of luxuriant white horsehair and wore finely crafted leather bridles and saddles, sometimes with

◄ *This rocking horse of 1890 is attached to a safety rocker, introduced in the 1880s in place of the bow rocker.* **8**

THE DAPPLED GREY

A fine example of the enduringly popular dappled grey rocking horse, this spirited creature was made in the late 19th century. Carved from wood, painted in bright colours and then varnished, it is mounted on a large bow rocker. Fitted with its original brown leather bridle, the horse has been given a new leather saddle and stirrups.

The glorious long mane of black horsehair is in good condition, covering the horse's head and neck. By comparison, the tail looks a bit sparse. The paintwork is in very good condition for a Victorian toy, with only minor chips on the legs, body and head, and – as would be expected – rather more on the rocker.

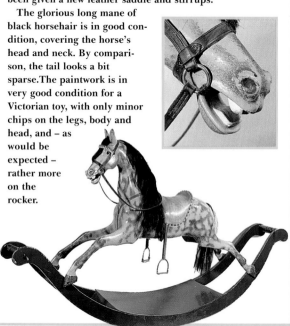

a fabric saddle-cloth. By the early 19th century, manufacturers were advertising rocking horses as desirable toys for children of both sexes. Girls, however, were expected to ride side-saddle. Some rocking horses were even fitted with a small wicker chair so that girls could rock with the decorum appropriate to a young lady. Attractive though the horse on its bow rockers was, the possibility of its

rocking right over when ridden too enthusi-
astically made it potentially unsafe for the
boisterous child.

The Trestle Support

In the 1880s, a safer platform was devised and
the rocking motion was replaced by a gentler
back and forth movement. The horse's legs
were attached to a pair of planks which swung
on metal brackets mounted on each end of a
trestle-like structure.

As well as making for a safer ride, trestle-
mounted rocking horses did not move about,
mark the floor or gouge holes in walls or
furniture. For all, however, bow rockers
are still considered the most attractive, with
their clean lines and prancing legs.

Leading Manufacturers

The first commercial manufacturers of rocking horses were probably the makers of fair-
ground gallopers. Such specialist firms also
made life-sized wooden horses for saddlers
and horses' heads to be displayed as pub signs.

The firm of G. and J. Lines began making
rocking horses in this way in the mid-19th
century. By the 1920s, G. and J. Lines, alongside their offshoot, Lines Bros. Ltd., were making a comprehensive range that included old-
style rocking horses on bow rockers, ingenious
'combination' horses which had wheels and
could be lifted on and off their
rockers, horses with me-
dieval-style trappings,
and quantities of the dappled greys on their safe
trestle stands. Other
notable manufac-
turers of the period

▼ *This tricycle horse*
dates from the 1870s. **8**

◀ *Real pony hide has been used to cover the wooden frame of this rocking horse dating from about 1880.* ❽

were the Liverpool Toy Industry, Woodrow & Co. of London and Norton & Baker of Birmingham. Early 19th-century makers included William Kain and William West.

The method of manufacture changed little over the years. The body was built up with as many as a dozen separate blocks of wood – usually pine or beech – roughly carved to the appropriate shape and either glued or tenoned together. After planing and sanding, the horse was painted with gesso to smooth over the joints, followed by a coat of white paint, the grey dapples and a coat of varnish. The mane, tail, saddle and bridle were added when the horse had been fixed to its rocker.

ᘒEALERS' TIPS

• **One of the most important features of a rocking horse is a good head. The eyes should be well defined, the ears pricked and the nostrils flared.**
• **Ideally the paintwork should be original. Even if it does show signs of wear, this is preferable to repainting.**
• **The mane and tail should be made of real horsehair and luxuriant. Check that they are firmly secured.**
• **The demand for rocking horses in good condition is such that they invariably fetch high prices. Superficial damage, such as a chip to the ears, is not regarded as a major flaw.**

MAGIC LANTERNS

THOUGH THEIR THRILLS MAY SEEM TAME TO THOSE BROUGHT UP IN THE VIDEO AGE, MAGIC LANTERNS WERE A SOURCE OF ENTERTAINMENT AND MYSTERY TO THEIR VICTORIAN AUDIENCES

T he idea of lighting an object from behind so that it casts a shadow on a wall or screen was developed in the Far East, where thin translucent puppets, painted with bright colours, acted out shadow plays on the wall. In Europe, no one saw the possibilities of back lighting until a Dutchman, Christiaen Huygens, invented a simple projector in 1649. The light source for these early lanterns was a candle or oil lamp, with a chimney fitted to stop it flickering.

Magic lanterns remained a popular curiosity until the Victorian period, when they really took off. Families bought their own lantern and slides, or hired an itinerant showman to perform in their living room. Lantern shows were popular public spectacles, too, set in draughty village halls or scientific institutions. Paraffin burners had been

◀ *This iron and brass lantern is one of many models made for children. It dates from the turn of the century and comes complete with its wooden box.* ❻

▲ *Dating from the late 19th century, this French praxinoscope has its original box and picture strips. The images reflected in the mirrors appear to move when the drum is spun round.* **8**

introduced to provide a steadier light, while the more intrepid showmen experimented with the unstable brilliance of limelight (lime was ignited by a combustible combination of sometimes volatile gases).

Nineteenth-century lanterns were sold at prices to suit every pocket. The most popular models were made of black tin-plate while enthusiasts on a limited budget could buy the lenses and build the casing themselves. Upmarket lanterns – advertised as fit for the drawing room – tended to be cased in mahogany or walnut, with brass fittings and an elaborate stand.

Victorian Magic

Some of the slides shown on the lanterns were hand-painted and some were made photographically, but it was the discovery of a way of mass-printing them in the 1850s that was responsible for their new wave of popularity. Various mechanical devices in the slide casings allowed the operator to give the illusion of movement, and experiments with magic lanterns laid the groundwork for the development of the cinema, which was largely responsible for the demise of the magic lantern after World War I.

▼ *This brass, iron and tin-plate lantern features a paraffin burner with an adjustable wick like an oil lamp.* **7**

*M*ECHANICAL SLIDES

By the use of levers and rotary handles, mechanical slides were able to give the illusion of movement. Magic lantern slides of all kinds are collectables in their own right and are sought after for their artistic merit or interesting subject matter rather than their functional value. Lovely hand-painted slides fall into price guide 4 or 5 for a set of eight. Attractive mass-produced ones are cheaper.

The most collectable Victorian lanterns are those with handsome wooden cases and shiny brass fittings, and those with some kind of optical sophistication. Look out for top brands such as Optimus, who specialized in lanterns made in Russian iron as well as mahogany, or Reynolds & Branson. They also made the so-called 'science lanterns'. These had room for experiments to take place between the lens and light source. A microscope attachment made them very useful teaching tools.

Biunial lanterns, developed towards the end of the century, had two lenses mounted one above the other, allowing the operator to 'dissolve' between one slide and the next. The true precursors of the cinema, relying on the

ℒANTERN SLIDES

Topics suitable for the family such as comic stories, religious and educational subjects were favourite lantern slide themes. Slides with humourous domestic scenes are particularly popular with collectors today and some charming images have survived. Hand-painted views – the most sought-after by collectors – gave way in the 1850s to mass-produced slides.

phenomenon of persistence of vision to create the illusion of movement, were led by Beale's choreutoscope of 1866, which allowed a sequence of slightly different images to be cranked past a small window in the lantern. Other optical toys that worked on this principle had splendidly unpronounceable names; the thaumatrope, the phenakistoscope, the praxinoscope and the zoetrope. Any of these in working order is of great interest to the modern collector.

After suffering an eclipse in the wake of World War I, the magic lantern has recently enjoyed a revival, and competitive, though not excessive prices are being paid for objects that were consigned to the dustbin not so long ago.

PLAYGROUND TOYS

*AFTER SCHOOL, VICTORIAN CHILDREN GATHERED TOGETHER TO
PLAY GAMES, OFTEN USING SIMPLE TOYS THAT ARE STILL POPULAR
WITH TODAY'S CHILDREN*

Simple outdoor toys have been around
for many hundreds of years. Boys in
Ancient Greece played with hoops and
tops, and Breughel's 16th-century paintings
show children playing with these two toys and
with hobby horses, dolls, skittles, marbles and
knuckle-bones. Many toys were of wood and
were carved by fathers and grandfathers; others were bought from pedlars or at fairs.

The simplest top was the twirler, a small
wooden top spun by twisting the stem between
the thumb and finger. Competitive games were
also played with peg tops – in the simplest version the child whose top went on spinning the

▲ *This skipping rope
has bells attached to
each handle. Wooden
handles were not commonplace until the early
years of this century.* ❹

longest won the game. To spin a peg top, the child wound string round the top and, holding on to the end, threw the top to the ground. The string unwound, spinning the top as it flew through the air to spin on the ground.

Skittles or ninepins were played by Victorian children of both sexes. The skittles were usually plain wooden pegs, but some were turned and painted soldiers . One advantage of skittles was that it could be played indoors, as could games such as ball-and-stick and ball-and-cup.

Victorian ingenuity was also applied to skipping ropes. Before the 19th century skipping ropes did not have handles – they were simply knotted at the ends. Wooden handles were added to make the rope easier to hold. In Yorkshire the handles were often made from the bobbins that were used in the wool mills.

Remarkably few children's toys from the 19th century survive today and, not surprisingly, fewer still are in first-class condition. Sophisticated spinning tops therefore fetch high prices. Simple handmade toys, such as hoops and skipping ropes, have a rarity value to the keen toy collector.

▲ *Made of lathe-turned wood, this ball and cup was made in the late 19th century.* ❹

◀ *This parachute top, by Jaques, the well-known toy manufacturer, is made of turned beech. It has a brass spindle and comes in its original box.* ❻

41

TEDDY BEARS

*ONCE JUST A NURSERY TOY RELEGATED TO THE ATTIC, TEDDY
BEARS ARE NOW CONSIDERED TO BE AMONG THE MOST
POPULAR OF ALL COLLECTABLES*

N o two teddy bears are the same, and
each one has a personality all its own,
as collectors will quickly tell you.
Although none will be strictly antique
until 2003, when the very first teddy
bears will reach the ripe old age of
100, they are now being treated with
the reverence usually associated with
fine objets d'art.

Teddy bears probably originated in
Giengen, Germany, at the stuffed toy factory of Margarete Steiff, although a similar toy was being developed in the
United States at the same time by the
Ideal Toy Company. The idea for mod-
elling a cuddly toy on bears came from
Steiff's nephew, Richard, who often
sketched bear cubs at Stuttgart
Zoo. The prototypes,
made in 1902, were the
first Steiff toys to have
moving limbs to make
them more realistic.

They were christened
'teddy' bears after the
then American President,
Teddy Roosevelt, who
had appeared in a famous

▶ *Today's collectors
can choose from a cen-
tury of teddy bears,
from the earliest ver-
sions to ones from all
over the world.*

cartoon in the Washington Post refusing to shoot a bear cub while on a hunt in Mississippi in 1902. From then on a bear became his mascot, and he was soon linked with the latest children's toy.

Early Teddy Bears

The new Steiff bears were exported to the United States and Britain in 1903 and people there quickly took them to their hearts. By 1907, the peak of what has become known as 'the bear years', Steiff's production had risen to almost a million bears a year and, by 1910, the teddy bear had become Britain's most popular toy by far. The earliest bears – those from the Edwardian

period – are most prized by collectors, even in the smaller sizes. Early bears are characterized by their long arms, curved paws, and exaggerated back humps. With long, pointed noses and glass or shoe-button eyes, they are made of soft mohair, with pads of leather, felt or plush. Claws, nose and mouth are usually embroidered in black or brown thread.

Steiff Bears

Early Steiffs are invariably the most desirable. An early Steiff in mint condition was auctioned at Sotheby's in London in 1989 for £55,000. Margarete Steiff registered the now-legendary metal button in the ear as a trademark in 1905, to reassure people that they were buying a genuine Steiff bear. But many old Steiffs have had their buttons pulled off, and few have survived intact. There are fake Steiffs around, but most experts can spot them a mile away. The most valuable Steiffs are the earliest, which have a pronounced muzzle, elongated limbs and a stitched nose.

Early bears over 66cm/2ft high and in very good condition sell for between £1200 and £6000. Other particularly desirable bears are those with makers' marks still attached or with some unusual feature, such as a turning head or

▲ *The hand-stitched nose on this bear suggests its early provenance: it is a Steiff bear dating from 1904.* **9**

◀ *This bear was made by Bing around 1913. If in working order, it performs somersaults and consequently commands a high price.* **9**

$\mathcal{F}$ACIAL FEATURES

By looking at a bear's features you can learn a great deal about when the bear was made and, ultimately, what the bear is worth, particularly if there is no mark.

Noses, like eyes, mouth and claws, have changed dramatically over the years. The more unusual noses, such as those in leather, are found on early bears. A hand-stitched nose in brown thread (*top*) also denotes an early date. Moulded rubber noses (*centre*) are found most commonly on bears from the 1950s, while today's bears usually have plastic noses (*bottom*) with a safety lock.

mechanical movements. Bears with growlers, which sound when the teddy is tipped backwards, date from 1908. These also add to the bear's value.

Modern Bears

In the 1920s and 1930s the British toy industry thrived and slowly but surely a new teddy bear shape began to emerge. These bears had less pronounced snouts, much shorter limbs and an ever-decreasing hump on the back.

Bears made in the 1950s and 1960s were distinctly different from those produced in earlier years. New safety standards brought many of these changes.

By 1955, when nylon plush coats and water-repellent fillings replaced natural materials, bears could even be kept clean with the occasional spin in the washing machine. It was during this period that British toy manufacturers were facing increased competition from American companies, whose cheaper labour costs meant

▼ *This Bing bear has a clockwork mechanism that enables him to play with the ball.* ❾

45

COMPARE & CONTRAST

Steiff c1904

Chad Valley c1930

Dean's c1960

**With his pronounced muzzle, long limbs and hump back, the
Steiff bear has a typical early shape. The Chad Valley bear
shows how the shape evolved – blunter muzzle, no hump and
shorter limbs. The still later Dean's bear has a floppy, shape-
less body, typical of later machine-made British bears.**

they could keep prices down. Most British companies produced machine-made bears, although some handmade teddies were produced for specialist collectors.

Modern bears were usually made in
synthetic fibres such as Bri-nylon or Acrilan
instead of mohair. Plastic was used for the eyes,
instead of glass or boot buttons. Kapok was
used for stuffing, replacing wood shavings or
sawdust, and velvet paw pads were replaced
by Rexine, an artificial leather.

Collectors' Tips

It is a good idea for the budding teddy bear
collector to browse around toy museums and
antiques fairs to get an idea of the variety of
bears available and to see what to look out for.

As a rule, the more unusual features the
bear has, the more valuable it is going to be,
although age and condition are obviously also
important factors. To determine a bear's manufacturer and likely age, look for any labels
or trademarks and examine physical characteristics, such as noses, limb length and back

▼ *This Schuco mechan-
ical walking bear is
dressed is his original
period clothes.* ❽

shape, since these have changed significantly over the years. Also look for signs of wear and tear, re-stuffing and replaced eye buttons and pads, which can reduce the value. Manufacturers worth looking out for are Chad Valley, Ideal Toy Company, Dean's, Hermann, Schreyer & Co., Merrythought and, of course, Steiff.

As the popularity of the teddy grows and grows, manufacturers have started producing bears specifically for the collector. Traditional jointed teddy bears are back in vogue, and they often appear in special costumes. The appeal of teddy bear characters from comics and television is reflected in the range of bears now available, such as Paddington, Robin Hood and Teddy Ruxpin. These, and the limited editions produced by Steiff and Hermann, will doubtless be the heirlooms of tomorrow.

▲ *Paddington Bear is now firmly established with collectors. This is one of the first, dating from the early 1950s.* **7**

𝒯RADE MARKS

Steiff was the first manufacturer to use a permanent identifying mark in 1905, but it took until the 1930s for most British manufacturers to follow suit. The trademarks can be found in a variety of materials and are attached to the body in a variety of ways.

An early Steiff button (*top*) has an embossed 'STEIFF' mark: some buttons were blank. The Chad Valley button has printed lettering. A modern Merrythought label is stitched and can be found on the right foot of the bear while the modern Steiff button (*bottom*) is sewn on to a tag.

CHILDREN'S BOOKS

THE GOLDEN AGE OF CHILDREN'S BOOK ILLUSTRATION COVERS THE CENTURY'S FIRST TWO DECADES, WHEN ARTISTS PRODUCED EXQUISITE COLOURED PLATES FOR CLASSIC FAIRY TALES AND NURSERY RHYMES

▶ *Margaret Tarrant was enormously popular in her time and illustrated many children's books. This one was published in 1914.* ❺

T he golden age of children's book illustration really took off in the last couple of decades of the 19th century when new printing techniques were able to reproduce as colour plates the delightful illustrations of now revered artists such as Arthur Rackham and Edmund Dulac. Rackham's most striking work was in his fantastic and slightly sinister depictions of Nordic legends. French-born Edmund Dulac was commissioned by Hodder & Stoughton to illustrate *Stories from the Arabian Nights*. His wonderful jewel-like illustrations won immediate acclaim. The same publisher also published the work of another celebrated foreigner, the Danish artist Kay Neilson, whose finest work was contained in *East of the Sun and West of the Moon*, a book of old tales from the North. Another foreigner popular in Britain was H. Willebeek Le Mair, a Dutch-born artist who created a

▼ *This page from a Lucie Attwell Annual dates from the 1940s.* ❸

◄ *This plate by Edmund Dulac is from his illustrations for Cinderella; it appeared in his* Picture Book for the French Red Cross, *published as a fundraiser in 1916.* ❺

series of delightful nursery rhyme illustrations. Mabel Lucie Attwell's sketches and paintings of chubby children made her hugely popular in the years up to and after World War I. Her books continued to be produced well into the 1940s.

Children's illustrated books from the first two decades of this century are no longer cheap. Books in good condition with plates by Rackham or Dulac are much sought after by collectors. Also pricey are children's books illustrated by W. Heath Robinson, largely due to his reputation as a cartoonist, while not far behind are works illustrated by Harry Clarke. These high prices are for first or early editions: reprints from the 1960s and 1970s are of little interest to the connoisseur.

However, it is still possible to find bargains. Anne Anderson is not well known, nor is the work of H. M. Brock or Lawson Wood. And, unlike Jessie Willcox Smith with whom she is sometimes compared, Margaret Tarrant books are often quite reasonably priced.

▲ *This edition of* Alice in Wonderland *dates from 1902 and is illustrated by John Tenniel.* ❸

EDWARDIAN PARLOUR GAMES

THE INNOCENT PASTIMES OF AN EDWARDIAN CHILDHOOD STILL HAVE THE POWER TO BEGUILE YOUNG AND OLD ALIKE

◀ *This compendium with chess, dominoes, cribbage board, draughts, backgammon and dice is of Edwardian origin.* ❽

▼ *This game of quoits, where hoops are tossed over pegs to score points, is a table-top version.* ❹

Anyone who has ever had to occupy their children while they were housebound by the lashing rain of an English summer will appreciate the importance of indoor amusements. Nowadays, television, video recorders and computer games usually fit the bill, but these were not available to Victorian and Edwardian households. There was also more leisure time for adults. The period between 1880 and the start of World War I was the heyday of parlour games.

There was a vast range of choice, from genteel board games to slightly more raucous pursuits. All were designed to appeal to children and adults alike. Middle-class families enjoyed long summer holidays, and no packing was complete without indoor games. Wood was a favoured material for lots of games and toys.

Richly coloured and figured woods such as beech, mahogany, Indonesian amboyna, walnut and rosewood were commonly used in making parlour toys. Their good looks make them excellent material for collection and display. Wooden solitaire boards, complete with pretty Nailsea marbles, are worth looking out for, as are miniature roulette wheels.

▲ *This mah-jong set has an amboyna box fitted with brass. The tiles are made of bone and bamboo.* **5**

A really good buy for games lovers would be a compendium games set. A complete one will have a good selection of games such as draughts, dominoes and chess, as well as boards, dice and dice cups to go with them. Good examples will be housed in a stout wooden box, possibly made of mahogany.

Among the most collectable games are ones which are still played today. Mah-jong, for example, has a wide following and old sets in good condition are much sought after. Very handsome sets may still be found with tiles made of bone and bamboo or even ivory.

Examine games that have lots of pieces very carefully before buying; missing items will reduce the value. Make sure, at the same time, that all the bits and pieces actually belong to the same set. It is not unusual for sets to be made up from various different sources but close examination should reveal impostors.

Games like table croquet, carpet bowls and mah-jong, as well as compendiums, were usually sold originally in handsome wooden boxes. Make sure that boxes and containers are perfect. The brass fittings – hinges, corners hooks and locks – should all be in good condition. It is essential that the box closes properly and that the key has not been turned and then lost.

▼ *Jigsaws of lithographed prints backed with softwood, rather than cardboard, were made for all ages.* **4**

MECHANICAL TOYS

INVENTIVE, WELL-CRAFTED METAL TOYS, POWERED BY CLOCKWORK OR SOME OTHER SIMPLE MECHANISM, DELIGHTED EDWARDIAN CHILDREN AND STRONGLY ATTRACT THE MODERN COLLECTOR

W orking models with clockwork motors, some of them enormously elaborate, were crafted for wealthy European patrons in the 18th and 19th centuries. However, it was not until the beginnings of mass-production in the latter half of the 19th century that mechanical toys came within the reach of children. Before 1895, all such toys were hand-painted. After that date, an increasing number of them were decorated with lithographic printing.

German Models

Germany was the centre of mechanical toy-making. The three most important firms were Bing of Nuremberg, founded in 1863, Märklin, established in Göppingen in 1859, and Ernst Paul Lehmann, which was based in Berlin. All three were mainly concerned with making tin-plate toys for the export market. Each company had its own distinctive style. Bing toys

▼ *This car was made by the German toymaker, Hess. It has a friction motor operated by the crank at the front, and a brake operated by the steering wheel.* **8**

PERFORMING TOYS

People and animals were second in popularity only to cars, trains and planes as subjects for mechanical tin-plate toys. One arena that provided a great deal of scope was the circus. Performing animals, tightrope walkers, trapeze artists and tumblers provided movement, while painted clowns supplied the merriment.

The tightrope walker *(right)* is a gravity-operated German toy of about 1900, while the clown riding a clockwork pig *(below)* is also German. As the pig wheels along, the pig's ears move and they in turn rock the clown.

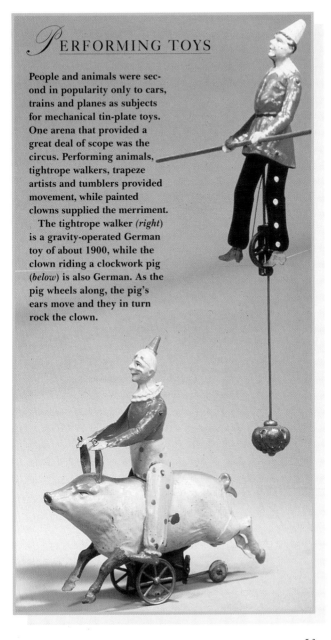

are noted for their solidity and attention to detail. Many of them were hand-painted, while the best of its cars also boasted opening doors and windows. Bing's ships were heavily constructed, had powerful motors and could perform some complicated manoeuvres.

Märklin made a vast range of toys. It is on their solidly-made model trains, cars and ships, among the finest ever produced, that the company's reputation largely rests today. Great emphasis was put on decorative and authentic detail. Export models were based on the real thing found in the importer's country.

By contrast, Lehmann's toys were flimsy and intentionally frivolous. Always cheap, Lehmann toys were decorated with colourful printing, and the parts were joined with tabs rather than soldered. The motors were cheap and insubstantial, with pressed tin-plate gears and spiral rather than coil springs.

Fun from France

Some French firms rivalled the Germans, though a much smaller proportion of their toys were exported, and they are consequently harder to find. Fernand Martin specialized in comical figures and animals. His appealing, if rather flimsy toys often satirized Parisian society. His range included servants juggling with piles of plates, a drunkard attempting to stay upright, and lawyers arguing their cases. Martin's figures were often dressed in fabrics, and so looked more realistic than painted toys.

Another French maker, Rossignol, also made cheap, ephemeral toys, and is chiefly remembered for being the first toymaker to include a model car in his range.

More than a decade ago it was possible to pick up novelty mechanical toys for a few pounds, but this is no longer the case. Even

▼ *This rowboat was made by Issmeyer. The clockwork motor moved the rower back and forth to operate the oars. The price is reduced by the missing oars and peeling paintwork.* ❼

DEALERS' TIPS

• Before buying, test that the mechanism works and that moving parts are in working order.
• If the key is missing, don't worry too much. They are standard sizes; most dealers will have a selection to try.
• Bing toys were marked 'G.B.N.' until 1919, and 'B.W.' from then until the factory closed in 1934. Lehmann and Märklin used the companies' full names. Rossignol toys are usually marked 'C.R.', and Martin's products 'F.M'.

ones which show some wear and tear can now fetch hundreds or even thousands of pounds if they are interesting pieces, carry the name of a well-known maker, or have some kind of musical movement. Cars, boats, trains and aeroplanes fall into specialist collectors' areas, and prices are particularly high. Any toy which has been played with will have scratches and minor damage and this is very acceptable; indeed, pieces in mint condition are rare.

MODEL BOATS

BEAUTIFULLY MADE BY TALENTED CRAFTSMEN, MODEL BOATS HAVE LONG BEEN ADMIRED AND PLAYED WITH BY ENTHUSIASTS OF ALL AGES

For the past 200 years model makers have produced replicas of 17th and 18th century British Navy Board vessels. In more recent years, they have turned their hands to cabin cruisers and ocean liners too. Before World War II, keen collectors could pick up rare finds among old shipwrights' models for next to nothing. Discarded working half-models of now extinct vessels were often left to decay unnoticed in boatyards' cellars or were simply used for firewood. Originally designed to show owners how their new boat was progressing, the earliest of these models dates from the late 16th century.

▲ *This fine wooden and metal replica of an early 19th-century schooner has one funnel and two masts. It is displayed in a case with a painted backdrop.* ❿

Skilfully Made

The once-famous 19th-century Blackwall frigates, and the glamorous clippers which traded in the Far East and Australia were sometimes recorded only in model form. The same is true of the many different kinds of regional vessel which plied British coasts. Few of these survived beyond the early years of the century, and shipping offices were happy to get rid of out-of-date replicas that had once depicted the pride of their fleets. Little valued then, these models now command prices that reflect the skill that went into making them.

Model kits did not come into their own until the 1950s, though there were some around in the 1930s. Between the wars, though, there were a

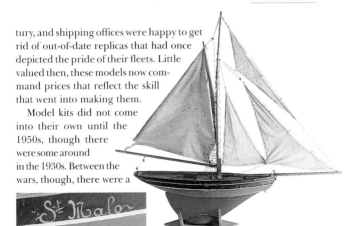

number of books to help model shipbuilders get started. Most dealt with British warships in the 1600s and 1700s.

In *The Built-up Ship Model*, published in 1933 and still in print, Charles G. Davis gave readers a sense of living in history by referring to 18th-century shipbuilders' manuals. And to give new model-makers confidence he advised starting with a 'relatively simple' replica of the *Lexington*, a single-deck American brig-o'-war fitted out in Philadelphia in 1775.

▲ *This Edwardian toy racing yacht is made of willow. The ship's name is painted on the side of the bow in neat gold lettering.* ❼

Model Ships

Enthusiasm for model ships has blossomed in the last decade. Many serious collectors are also keen model builders, able to restore to their former glory damaged replicas that they have picked up in junk shops or boatyards.

During World War II a large proportion of the ship models in European museum collections were destroyed by bombing. In England too, many were lost, including relics from Drake's voyages and a superb model made in the 17th century when Samuel Pepys was employed as Surveyor of the Navy. Large model liners were often used by shipping offices to advertise their cruises. Encased in glass, they showed minute details of the superstructure and differed from the Navy Board

▼ *This finely crafted model yacht was made in the 1930s. It has a wooden deck with a planking finish.* ❽

models only by being solid inside. As ever larger and more glorious liners were built, the old models were replaced with new ones. The discarded ones were left virtually untouched until recent years. Now they are being sought after once again as decoration for offices, restaurants, pubs and other public buildings.

Sailing Boats

Toy wooden boats and yachts were beautifully designed and made, and are attractive to today's collectors. The most common ones were the racing yachts meant to be used on boating ponds. These were made by such firms as Bassett-Lowke, Triang and other less well-known companies.

Smaller wooden 'basin boats' designed for use in the bath were also popular, but they were mostly very simple in design and are not considered valuable today. An exception to this rule are models of ferryboats and liners carved by George Scott which can fetch substantial prices at auction.

Collectors' Notes

Specialist dealers generally cover the range of model ships, from models of frigates and ocean liners, to fishing boats

MODELLERS' DETAILS

Some models are master-
pieces of detailed work-
manship. Rigging is accu-
rately reproduced with fine
cord and the sail stamped
with the name of the sail
design or the name of the
boat's class (*right*). In place
of a tiller, the model (*below*)
has a steering mechanism
linked to a pulley that con-
trols the rigging of the
sails. The deck rope (*below
right*) is in a classic coil.

and even yachts complete with rope bindings,
anchors, bollards and deck rails.

Many of the 17th and 18th century models were heavily restored at the start of the
20th century and these should be avoided
because they are often full of stylistic anachro-
nisms. This is especially true of American
replicas, but clumsy repairs were often made
on British ones as well.

The original Navy Board models were mas-
terpieces of technology involving a team of
expert carvers, artists and specialists in
miniature metalwork, as well as the shipwrights themselves. Tiny hinges and filigree
work may have been carried out by watch-
makers and jewellers. It is virtually impossible to re-create their skills today and no one
but an expert should attempt repairs.

TOY TRAINS

THE ROMANCE OF THE RAILWAYS AND NOSTALGIA FOR INNOCENT BOYHOOD PLEASURES HAVE MADE TRAIN SETS AMONG THE MOST COLLECTABLE OF TOYS

R ailways, and particularly steam railways, have from the very first attracted the enthusiasm of boys and their fathers. Toy makers in England, France and Germany were quick to see the possible appeal of toy trains.

The first great name in the field was the German firm, Märklin, who produced a figure-of-eight track in the 1890s. They are still in business today. Their locomotives, carriages, stations and accessories have always been treasured; old ones fetch fantastic prices. Märklin, and their German rivals, Bing, always had

▲ *The green locomotive and tender, made by Mettoy in 1937, appear alongside the streamlined model of an American train made by Lionel Lines. The price guide reads from top to bottom and includes coaches for both locomotives.* ❹ ❻

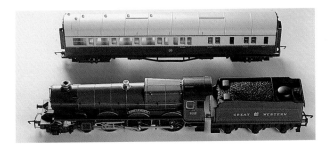

high standards, but the most accurate scale models were produced by an Englishman, W. J. Bassett-Lowke.

The accuracy of model trains was sometimes hampered by the need to include a clockwork or steam engine to power them. This problem was solved with the introduction of electric train sets in 1898. Early electric models were powered by mains electricity at a dangerous 120 volts. By the 1920s, though, transformers had been developed that reduced the power to a more acceptable 20 volts. Before World War I, locomotives were generally made of printed tin-plate, though later ones tended to be made of die-cast metal.

Train sets were often regarded as special toys and treated with great care. This means that a remarkable number of them have survived in good condition.

▲ *This GWR locomotive and first-class carriage are modern versions of Hornby Dublo's model trains.* **5**

𝒟EALERS' TIPS

- **Locomotives and tenders fetch the highest prices.**
- **Sets made by Märklin, Bing or Bassett-Lowke can be fantastically expensive.**
- **Sets made by Hornby are now also very collectable but more reasonably priced.**
- **Condition is paramount in setting the price of an old model train.**
- **Colourful rolling stock is very desirable, especially coaches and wagons with inscriptions.**

TOY SOLDIERS

A SET OF WELL-MADE, HAND-PAINTED METAL TOY SOLDIERS WERE ALWAYS AN ACCEPTABLE PRESENT FOR BOYS. TODAY THEY ARE COLLECTED BY MILITARY ENTHUSIASTS AND WAR-GAMERS

Model soldiers in tin and lead survive from the 16th century, but it was only in the 18th century that they were produced in great numbers. The first mass-produced soldiers were tin and moulded flat, so they were easily broken. Towards 1800, French and German manufacturers began making three-dimensional models in solid lead, with a little tin and antimony. Some were of very high quality and quite expensive.

In 1893, an English firm, Britains, developed a new technique, hollowcasting. Molten lead was poured into a mould, then out again, leaving behind a hollow shell that became the model. The saving on raw materials brought down prices. Britains prospered and several other firms began making hollowcast toys.

The company's full range included knights in armour and cowboys and Indians, but their mainstay was a variety of British and foreign soldiers in battledress or dress uniform, painted in up to 12 colours. They came in sets, usually five

▼ *Though not as common as soldiers, toy sailors are just as collectable.* ❹

▲ *This bugling Britains' guardsman was issued in 1910, while the boy piper dates from 1936.* ❹

◀ *This cavalryman was made by one of Britains' competitors, John Hill. The Britains' version costs three times more.* ❹

mounted or eight foot soldiers to a box, and were made until 1966. Avidly collected, they now have specialist magazines, auctions and dealers devoted to them.

Fighting Men

Soldiers made by Britains dominate the market. They are easily recognized, as all have the manufacturer's stamp on the base. In the Edwardian period, several pirate copies of Britains' models were produced. These will only fool the unpracticed eye; they tend to be in a brighter metal, have rough edges and thinner paint than the real thing.

As a rule, sets are worth more than individual figures, and sets in their original boxes are worth most of all. The most valuable is a set in mint condition that has never been removed from its box – an original box may even double a set's value. Not all collectors insist on models in good condition; wargamers may well retouch or repaint models themselves.

If models are kept in a cabinet, it should be well-ventilated and not made of oak; damp and tannic acid, secreted by oak, both cause lead to deteriorate.

▼ *This motorcycle despatch rider, also by John Hill, was made around the beginning of World War II.* ❹

BAKELITE TOYS

*THE INVENTION OF BAKELITE PRESENTED DESIGNERS WITH A NEW
MATERIAL WHOSE PROPERTIES LENT THEMSELVES TO INNOVATIVE
AND EXCITING TOYS THAT SUITED THE STYLE OF THE 20TH CENTURY*

The revolutionary material Bakelite was invented in 1907 in the United States by a Belgian-born chemist, Leo Baekeland, who filed his manufacturing patent for this synthetic plastic in 1909. Made from a mixture of disinfectant and alcohol pre-server, it was known technically as phenol-formaldehyde resin, but was commonly called phenolic resin or Bakelite. It was often mixed with wood flour filler and sometimes coloured with extracts of coal or tar to simulate various types of wood.

The resin was poured into a metal mould and subjected to high tem-peratures and pressures to shape it and form a solid material. Initially, it was used as an electrical insulator but it soon began to take on other func-tions and was moulded into radio casings, telephones, heat-resistant handles for kitchen utensils, picnic sets, jewellery and various toys.

▲ *This roulette wheel is
a sturdy example in
marbled Bakelite.* ⑤

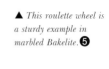

◀ *A version of poker
could be played on
this American-made
Prohibition machine.* ⑤

With the advent of Bakelite it was possible to create a rich new range of curvaceous and bulbous designs that would never have been mass-produced in wood or metal. Its properties were to bring about mass consumerism in easily manufactured and therefore relatively low-cost goods.

▲ *This Bakelite car is a replica of the Golden Arrow that set the 1929 land speed record.* **9**

Bakelite toys are sometimes striking in both design and colour and are much sought after. They were produced in many countries, as far apart as Australia and Czechoslovakia, from the mid-1920s up until the late 1940s.

The facility with which Bakelite could be moulded into any shape made it an ideal material for gambling machines. In the USA during the Prohibition years (1919-1933) gambling was outlawed. Small gambling machines, such as pocket 'Put & Take' and mini fruit machines, therefore became all the rage. Wherever gambling did take place, roulette wheels, dice-throwing baskets and gaming chips were often made of Bakelite. Classic games like draughts and dominoes all enjoyed a new lease of life with pieces in Bakelite.

▼ *This pocket version of roulette was an American 'Put & Take' game called Autogiro.* **5**

Highly detailed working models of planes, trains and automobiles were produced. The wonderfully streamlined Golden Arrow racing car is a specially good example. These and many other Bakelite toys were not always manufactured in great quantities and, allowing for the deep unpopularity of Bakelite in the 1960s and 1970s as well as its tendency to both crack and chip, can only mean that a good example is rare.

HARD PLASTIC DOLLS

BETWEEN 1946 AND 1956, THOUSANDS OF DIFFERENT DOLLS IN HARD PLASTIC MOULDINGS WERE MADE. THEY ARE ALREADY ATTRACTING SERIOUS COLLECTORS

D uring World War II, the majority of British toy companies devoted most of their capacity to war work, and perfected the use of 'hard plastic' (cellulose acetate) in making aircraft parts. When the war was over, they began making dolls from this new material, rather than composition (sawdust, water and animal glue), which had been used in the 1930s. Hard plastic was better suited to injection moulding techniques, and the parts could be poured, dried and seamed together without long drying-out periods and specialist painting. Hard plastic gave a pleasing shiny finish and crisper definition to features such as noses and ears.

About ten major toy companies made hard plastic dolls. This was a great period in toymaking, as the post-war baby boom generation was indulged by parents enjoying greatly increased prosperity.

In the beginning, the new dolls were gradually introduced in small sizes – 7.5cm/3in to 30cm/12in tall. These early dolls generally had arms that swung from the shoulder, a fixed head and legs, painted or painted tin sleep-

▲ *A smart home-made outfit in the style of the the early 1960s enhances this Pedigree knee-joint doll of 1959.* **5**

◀ *These four dolls, almost identical save for their hair, were made, from left to right, by Rosebud, Amanda Jane, Faerie Glen and Roddy. They all fall within the same price range.* **4**

*M*AKERS' MARKS

The great majority of hard plastic dolls carried their makers' names between their shoulder blades, inscribed in the moulds that made them. Four top makers from the 1950s are shown here: Tudor Rose, Palitoy, Pedigree and Sarold. Of these, Pedigree and Palitoy are the most collectable.

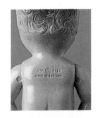
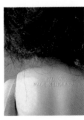

ing eyes, and moulded, painted hair. Soon, though, they became more realistic, with five moveable joints, painted plastic sleeping eyes with lashes, and a glued-on mohair wig.

Distinguishing Features

There was great rivalry between the various companies to produce the most beautiful, most realistic, and lightweight dolls. Each company's dolls had their special characteristics. Pedigree's had slightly shorter arms, while Roddy dolls had clenched fists with their thumbs raised. Palitoy dolls had slightly shorter legs than their rivals, and Rosebud, appropriately, had tiny rosebud mouths.

◄ *These dolls are both Roddy dolls with painted eyes and moulded plastic hair.* ❸

Generally, though, manufacturers used very similar styles, marketing techniques and packaging, and relied on annual innovations to get a larger share of the market.

Endless variations were created from a few favourite head moulds. Brushable Saran nylon wigs were introduced in as many as six colours. Various styles including short, straight, curly, fringed, centre-parted, plaited and waved were created. Glassene sleeping eyes were introduced, and there were bent limb babies, straight leg girls, walking mechanisms and knee joint dolls. Named dolls created cults of their own. Outfits changed regularly, too, and patterns for new clothes were regularly printed in women's magazines.

▼ *The regal costume suggests that this Roddy doll may have been dressed in 1953, the year of the coronation.* ❸

Hard Bargains

The beginning of the end for hard plastic dolls was in 1956, when the first dolls made of vinyl – soft plastic – came onto the market.

ℬLACK DOLLS

Before the 1950s, black dolls were made to represent African national costume. It was only from 1951, when immigrants arrived from the West Indies, that black plastic dolls were made. They were discontinued in 1959 and are hard to find today, due to the small number made.

A combination of size, rarity, condition and popularity sets the price of hard plastic dolls. Pedigree, Rosebud and Palitoy are the most collectable brands. They are more sought after and more expensive than other companies which closely followed their style – Roddy, Sarold, Tudor Rose or Williams & Steer.

Whatever their make, dolls which have unusual or special characteristics and were made in comparatively small numbers have greatly increased in price since the beginning of the 1990s.

POST WAR TOY CARS

*ORIGINALLY SOLD AS POCKET-MONEY TOYS, MINIATURE MODELS
IN CARDBOARD BOXES NOW ATTRACT COLLECTORS FROM
ALL OVER THE WORLD*

◀ *This clockwork car
was made in Germany
by Schuco. The driver
turns his head and
raises his arms.* **5**

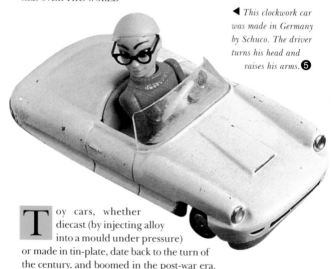

Toy cars, whether
diecast (by injecting alloy
into a mould under pressure)
or made in tin-plate, date back to the turn of
the century, and boomed in the post-war era.

Tin-plate clockwork cars were produced
by companies such as Tipp, Gunthermann
and Paya. In the 1950s, the Japanese share
of the battery-operated tin-plate toy market
gradually overtook that of the Germans. By
the 1960s, Japan had become the world's
largest manufacturer of battery-operated toys. Many of these toys were
copies of American vehicles.

▼*This Corgi model is
of a Heinkel car from
the 1960s. The price in-
cludes the box.* **3**

Diecast Cars

Frank Hornby (who founded
Meccano in 1901) introduced
small diecast cars in 1934. He sold
them first as accessories to his
model railways, but the Dinky cars, as

◄ *This American Ford dates from 1951 and was made by Haji of Japan. Like most tin-plate cars, it was sold unboxed.* ❺

they were called, were an instant hit in their own right. Meccano's Dinky series held a monopoly until the 1950s, when many new companies threatened their hold on the market. European manufacturers also began producing quality cars during this decade.

Lesney launched their Matchbox cars in 1953, closely followed by Mettoy's Playcraft Toys with their Corgi range in 1956. In 1965 Lesney introduced their Models of Yesteryear series.

In the late 1960s, the American company Mattel produced their Hot Wheels cars. These had low-friction axles which allowed

ℬASE PLATES

Corgi (*left*) were Dinky's major rival. As competition increased, manufacturers began to include details of patents on the stamped base plates (*centre*).The post-war base plate of the German maker Schuco includes a piece of history in its country of origin stamp (*right*).

*D*EALERS' TIPS

• **Windscreens and working parts first appeared in the 1950s, and 1959 saw wheels made of aluminium.**
• **Names to look out for include Triang's Spot-On series, Corgi, Britains, Timpo, Solido, Dinky and Matchbox.**
• **Early Dinky cars bore the name 'Meccano', sometimes placed in an obscure position.**
• **The most collectable foreign diecast cars are Märklin and Siku, both from Germany.**

them to be pushed along the floor at high speeds or to whizz along a flexible plastic track. Other manufacturers copied the idea, but their products were often inferior to the original.

The 1960s is considered to be the great decade for diecast cars. Manufacturers, realizing the potential market for adult collectors, began paying greater attention to detail. Doors and other opening parts of the car had previously been cut into the mould, showing in relief on the finished item. This method was now improved although, as early as 1956, Corgi cars had been advertised on television as being 'the ones with the windows'. Collectors generally agree that the 1970s should be the terminal date for collecting. Apart from the Matchbox Yesteryear models, the heyday of diecasts ended then.

◄ *This Austin Somerset saloon from the 1950s was an early Dinky toy. It has no seats or windows but comes with its original box.* ❹

MATCHBOX TOYS

In 1953, the firm of Lesney – the name was created by joining the two Christian names of its founders, Leslie and Rodney Smith – began making diecast cars small enough to fit in a matchbox. The idea soon caught on and by the 1960s Lesney were making more than five million models a week. New models continued to be made until number 75 was reached. The Hillman Minx (*right*) was No. 43 in the 1–75 Series Regular Wheels, which was produced between 1953 and 1969. The car has plastic windows and grey rubber composition wheels. It comes in its original box.

The first criterion in collecting toy cars is good condition. Wear and tear from their young owners drastically reduces the value of many vehicles. Restoration and repainting also lower the value enormously. Some collectors, however, will buy rare examples and repaint them for their own pleasure. The box in which the car was sold is of extreme importance and greatly increases the value if it is in pristine condition. It is worth remembering, though, that pre-war cars were never boxed. Dinky cars manufactured before 1950 were also sold without boxes.

Tyres frequently went missing when the car was played with, but these can often be bought from specialist shops. However, check for replacement parts when buying cars as they will reduce the value. These parts are usually brighter than the original. The white metal used is soft and bends easily under pressure.

▼ *This Lipton's tea van is a Models of Yesteryear piece from the 1970s.* ❷

BARBIE DOLLS

ONE OF THE MORE RECENT ARRIVALS ON THE COLLECTABLES SCENE, BARBIE, WITH HER FABULOUS FASHIONS, IS HERE TO STAY

Dolls have long been a popular subject for collectors, but today it's not only gorgeously gowned Victorian china dolls which command good prices. As the children of the 1960s and 1970s grow into adulthood, the vinyl fashion dolls or dress-up dolls of their youth, such as Sindy, Tressy, Tina and their American cousin, Barbie, are increasingly sought after.

Barbie – probably the most famous doll ever made – was the brainchild of Mr and Mrs Elliott Handler of the American company, Mattel. First sold in 1959, Barbie was named after the Handlers' daughter. She was one of the first teenaged dolls to appear on the market.

▼ *Barbie was such a moneymaker that Mattel created a vast social network for her. As well as cousins, friends and a younger sister (front row, right), the most enduring was her boyfriend Ken (back row, centre).*

Barbie had – to begin with – 22 beautifully made outfits which were, to many people, the most appealing thing about her. By the following year she had become a great success in the States, and Mattel introduced more outfits for her, as well as a boyfriend – named Ken after the Handlers' son.

◀ *This carrying case dates from the early 1960s.* ❹

Barbie soon became a multi-million-dollar industry: Mattel produced a huge family of friends and relations; pet animals; hundreds of outfits; houses, theatres and shops; aeroplanes and sailing boats; a swimming pool and an 'Olympic Gymnast' set, not to mention a board game and a 'Barbie Sings!' record.

The Fashion Model

Barbie was created as a young fashion model with a voluptuous figure. Her rooted hair (either blonde or brunette) was pulled up into a long ponytail with a short, curly fringe. She was sold wearing gold hoop earrings, a black and white striped strapless swimsuit and black plastic high-heeled sandals, and carried a pair of white sunglasses with blue lenses.

Fashion Parade

Barbie had annual makeovers in order to keep up with the times. The pointed eyebrows and white irises of the first models – Numbers 1 and 2 – changed to curved eyebrows and blue irises by 1960. Her bright red lipstick and nail polish became soft pink on some dolls in 1962, and in the same year she got a new red, round-necked swimsuit.

The year 1964 welcomed 'Miss Barbie' with bendable legs and eyes that shut. Barbie 'Color Magic', introduced in 1966, had treated hair and clothes that could change colour with the application of a special solution. In 1967 Barbie

▼ *This Barbie doll is model Number 3 and dates from 1960.* ❼

got a new, more girlish face, real eyelashes and a 'twist 'n turn' waist, and in 1968 she learned to talk. In 1969 she got a new 'flip' hairstyle with a long, side-swept fringe, but she soon tired of setting her hair every night, and by the following year it was straight, with an eyebrow-length fringe. In 1971 Barbie's eyes were painted looking straight ahead – on earlier dolls, they had looked to the right. By the next year she had hair that grew and hands that could hold things. The changes went on and on....

Collectors' Notes

The most valuable Barbie is undoubtedly Number 1 – in unopened packaging she could fetch £1000 or more. She can be identified by the holes in the balls of her feet (and in her sandals) which enable her to pose on a two-pronged black stand. Number 2 is worth almost as much and is exactly the same, except that she no longer has holes in her feet, and her posing stand has a wire to hold her up instead of prongs. A few of these dolls have pearl earrings instead of hoops. Look out for the following characteristics to identify 1 and 2: pointed eyebrows; eyes with white irises; pale skin; stock number 850; torso marked 'Barbie TM Pats Pend © MCMLVIII by Mattel Inc'.

◀ *This Barbie wears one of her most famous outfits, 'Solo in the Spotlight'.* ❺

Though millions of Barbies have been manufactured since 1959, most have been treated as the much-loved playthings that they were intended to be, and you would be lucky indeed to find one of the first models in mint condition.

The Perfect Doll

If you do manage to find an early doll in unopened packaging, its value will be greatly increased; such a doll could be worth more than ten times what a nude doll, even in good condition, would fetch. Similarly, outfits in sealed packets are the most desirable.

Various defects will reduce a doll's value. Look out for marks or stains; worn paint on face or nails; missing fingers, eyelashes or earrings, and hair that has been cut or rearranged. Check that the doll's head and body are of the same shade and type of plastic – a difference indicates that the parts have been assembled from different models. Store your Barbie dolls without their shoes, earrings and wigs; all can cause staining or distortion if left for a long time.

▲ *Barbie's Suburban Shopper outfit dates from 1959–1964.* ❹

▼ *This room setting shows a sampling of 1960s' accessories..*

ACTION MAN FIGURES

BEFORE THE 1960S, IT WAS THOUGHT IMPOSSIBLE TO SELL DOLLS TO BOYS, BUT ACTION MAN, UNDENIABLY MACHO AND VIRTUALLY INDESTRUCTIBLE, CHANGED ALL THAT

T o toy manufacturers, the dress-up doll was a marketing godsend. Once they had sold the basic doll, they had a captive market for the various outfits and accessories – even furniture – they produced for them. The only problem was that they were only reaching half the children – just the girls.

Then, in 1964, the American firm, Hasbro, produced GI Joe, a soldier doll that boys could play with without being taunted by their peers. Two years later, Palitoy, the British firm that created Tressy, launched Action Man. The secret of his success was his flexibility; jointed at the neck, shoulders, waist, elbows, hips, knees,

▼ *Action Man is seen here in a range of outfits: as a soldier, a sailor and as a member of a polar expedition. The price guides read from left to right.* ❸ ❹ ❹